# A PRAYER ON ENTERING

*The Healer's Hearth a Sanctuary*

# A PRAYER ON ENTERING

## The Healer's Hearth a Sanctuary

## JOHN DIAMOND, M.D.
### D.P.M., F.R.A.N.Z.C.P., M.R.C.Psych.

## Other Books by Dr. John Diamond:

*Your Body Doesn't Lie*

*Life Energy: Unlocking the Hidden Power of Your Emotions to Achieve Total Well-Being*

*Life-Energy Analysis: A Way to Cantillation*

*The Re-Mothering Experience: How to Totally Love*

*The Life Energy in Music (The Life Energy in Music, Volume I)*

*The Wellspring of Music (The Life Energy in Music, Volume II)*

*The Heart of Music (The Life Energy in Music, Volume III)*

*A Spiritual Basis of Holistic Therapy*

*The Collected Papers, Volumes I and II*

*Speech, Language and the Power of the Breath*

*A Book of Cantillatory Poems*

**All books available from:**

The Diamond Center
P.O. Box 381
South Salem, New York 10590 USA

A PRAYER ON ENTERING
*The Healer's Hearth a Sanctuary*
Copyright ©1997 by John Diamond, M.D.

Published by     Creativity Publishing
                 P.O. Box 381
                 South Salem, NY 10590

Printed in the United States of America

ISBN 1-890995-00-2

*To all those*
*who have come and sat beside me at the hearth*
*and to those yet to come*

# To the Reader

This little book is an essay, in the old sense of the word — a trial or an experiment. It is a trial, an attempt, to delineate my concept of the healer himself, as well as his environment, as a sanctuary.

And my healing practice is an experiment to determine whether I can bring this concept into reality.

I look at you, into you, to see the Perfection that is you — the being you aspire to become. And I try to help you to find This, and to find It in your mother: the Mother she wanted to be.

I ask you to do the same with me.

I use words like *love* and *spirit* freely in my writings. And this invites judgment. But try to see me not as I am, not as I do — but as I really am: the being I aspire to become.

> The cure starts
> when the sufferer
> sees the healer
> as human.

————

*Come hither, be patient. Let us converse together,*
*because I also tremble at myself and all my former life.*

BLAKE

I open my heart
to receive your pain.
Come,
come inside.

# A Prayer On Entering

*L*et us imagine that you are going to enter a Sanctuary, a holy place of refuge where you will feel safe and loved.

There you can at last become your true and deepest Self. There you will at last realize that you, and everyone, are Perfection. There you will become grateful for your suffering for it has brought you to this Sanctuary of Healing.

As we pass along the passageway, let us imagine we are about to enter not a room but a sphere — a Sphere of Love, of Belovedness.

Now let us enter with this imagining.

Within this Sanctum Sanctorum we will love each other — but not as ourselves. I will imagine that you are as my mother, my mother at her most loving — the Mother she always desired to be. And I will encourage you to do the same with me.

Through each other we will discover the Belovedness of our own mothers. And it is only in this State of Belovedness that true Healing can take place.

For only then is the Life Energy, the Love, the Healing Power, actuated strongly. Only when we feel Beloved by our mothers can we fully embrace health and life.

Imagine both of us loved. And loving — initially our mothers, and then the whole world as our mothers.

And let us imagine that when you leave the Sphere of Belovedness, passing down the passageway to the outer world, everything and everyone will seem changed. You will have changed — permanently. Imagine that you will have found Heaven on earth. And that you will now live accordingly.

For everywhere you will feel the Love, the glory of Existence.

———

Enter my home,
enter into me.
I open myself
to your suffering.

The sufferer's soul
a quivering dove
which he gives
into my hands
for me to help it
fly.

# The Healer

$\mathcal{I}$ would like to consider my profession as being what Freud called "a new profession of secular minister of the soul."

But instead of just minister, which can also have religious connotations, rather a healer. A healer of the soul suffering, a healer of the spirit. Not a spiritual healer, for I don't think of myself as healing by spirit, but instead helping a sufferer overcome his pain by encouraging the workings of the Healing Power of his own Spirit, which I refer to as his Life Energy.

But before I can help him heal himself, help him invoke his Spirit, his Healing Power, he must ask himself at his deepest level, if he really wants to be healed. The clearer he is of the exact nature of his suffering, the easier it will be for him to be healed.

A major part of my work is to help him to go into himself, deeply, honestly. To find the precise fulcrum point of his pain. Once we do, it is so easy to tip the balance for life and love.

I can openly speak of love in the therapeutic situation, for it has nothing to do with the healer personally, nor the sufferer.

All the love is mother-surrogate.

To the healer, the sufferer is his mother to whom he gratefully returns her Love. And to the sufferer, the healer is his mother from who he receives Love and now gives It back in grateful return.

I prefer the word *healer* to *therapist*, because it sounds less medical. For a doctor of medicine to call himself a healer implies a renunciation of the modern medical model, and this I heartily volunteer.

On the other hand, healer runs the risk of becoming treater. Healer is from the Indo-European root *kallo*, whole. A healer can see himself as being the restorer of health, of wholeness. But then he is as grandiose as a treater, placing himself above, even ignoring, the Healer within, the sufferer's Life Energy.

But if the healer acknowledges and reverences the sufferer's deep drive for Wholeness and desires to assist It, then he is a True Healer.

And a True Healer is a True Holistic Therapist — all of his Self is at the service of all the Powers within the sufferer yearning to be expressed.

A True Therapist does not order or dictate, for he is a servant of the sufferer's Life Energy. He recommends, suggests, and encourages — as humbly as he can.

A True Therapist, a True Healer, does not diagnose, treat or prescribe in any medical sense. For he is concerned not with disease but, much more importantly, with Life Energy.

He is a minister, tending to the needs of the impaired Healing Powers of the sufferer.

Thus he is, I believe, a member of Freud's "new profession of minister of the soul."

———————

To the souls
I have ministered,
I dedicate this place,
sanctified
by their suffering.

# The Healer's Environment

*I* worked hard to graduate into Medicine, and harder and longer to graduate out of it — as it has become. I will always have my university degree, but I long ago ceased to be a doctor. I am a healer.

I do not diagnose or treat disease. I wear no white coat or stethoscope, have no medical suite, accept no medical insurance — and want no patients.

Instead, I want those who want me to help them raise their Life Energy, their own Healing Power — those who realize this is the only true path to alleviate their suffering. To them I bring all my experience in medicine and psychiatry — and life. But as a holistic healer, not a medical doctor.

But, I've often wondered, how do I set up the right image for my healing practice so that the new sufferer knows what to expect, and thus how to best help me to help him?

Should I have not a clinically white door proclaiming "John Diamond, M.D." but instead a screen of colored beads? Should he enter through them not into a sterile treatment room with medical instruments and apparati, but into a Bedouin tent or a Japanese teahouse?

And should I wear not a white coat but a Joseph multicolored gown, or one like the Therapeutae?

None of the above!

But how to give a clearer image of what together we are going to do?

The appurtenances don't matter. All superficial, all pretense. The essential is what I create within my room, within my home.

A place of peace — a Quiet Place — where the sufferer may, hopefully, come to Know his Love, his Perfection, his Buddha nature. For only This can truly alleviate his suffering.

And the stronger this becomes my Intention, the surer will the approaching sufferer know me and my work. For it will emanate from my room, from my home, to him wherever he may be.

———————

# Hearth, Heart, Home —
# And Healer

*I*, as a healer, try to make my home a hearth, where the Life Energy, the Heart Flame, the flame of Love and Life, of the sufferer may be rekindled to blaze anew.

The word hearth is derived from the root *ker*, meaning heat or fire and thus a hearth is "a fireplace, a furnace, family life, the home." Let's consider some of the associations to *hearth*.

### Heat and Heart

"The heart is the hearth from whence proceedeth all heate."

### Home

"An environment offering security and happiness; a valued place regarded as a refuge."

"Hearth and home."

"The hearth was in the centre of the home."

### Family

"The joys of family and hearth."

"The hearth was in the centre of the family."

## *Altar*

"Their hearths and altars."

"The altar is a magnified kitchen-hearth."

"In the private house [in Ancient Rome] the hearth supplied the place of the altar."

"The centre of Greek life was the domestic hearth, also regarded as a sacrificial altar."

## *Sacred fire*

"Vesta — the goddess of hearth and household."

"Worshipped in a temple containing the sacred fire."

"The sacred fire which was kept constantly burning in the public hearth... was taken from the altar of Vesta."

## *Hearth–Heat–Heart–Heart Aflame–Altar–Sacred Fire — and Home.*

May the flame of Love and Life of the sufferer be rekindled to blaze anew in my hearth, my home.

> *And if any enter into thee,*
> *thou shalt be an Unquenchable Fire.*
>
> BLAKE

Although I refer to my room, my home, my hearth, I try not to think of them possessively.

But rather I accept responsibility for this little piece of earth and habitation — to clean it, protect it, and, most of all, consecrate it.

I am its sexton and priest, shammes and rabbi.

———————

*A* healer once told me that another equally gifted healer identified her unmarked home on entering the street because of the aura it emanated.

I wish that my home were like that — the healing aspiration expanding ever more outward into the environs.

I sometimes imagine that it has two outspread arms, open wide.

———

*I* find it fascinating that the words *host* and *guest* have the same origin, both derived from the Indo-European root *ghostis*, a stranger. They are so intertwined that the Latin *hostis* (from the *ghostis* root) means a stranger or a guest.

So stranger, guest and host are all related in our unconscious. They all relate "to someone with whom one has reciprocal duties of hospitality." And *hospitality* is also from the same root.

We meet at my door as strangers, I the host, you the guest. And we each have "reciprocal duties of hospitality" — to be "favorably receptive and open."

May we, through our meeting, come to the reciprocal recognition of the Oneness. There are no strangers.

———————

Each interaction
creates a vibration
in the room.

Day after day,
I try to make
them harmony,
silent, ever ascending.

*Joe* Heaney, the great traditional Irish folksinger, once told me that when he was young his family would in the evening sit around the peat fire in the parlor and each in turn would sing. The songs they chose were, he said, told to them by the fire — the patterns of the flames would suggest one, and then another.

That's the way to sing — inspired by the flames in the hearth.

That's what I'd like us to do. To sit at the hearth, and be inspired.

Maybe we'd sing. Maybe silent. We might seem to be just sitting — but it'd be so much more. We'd be Aspiring.

———

Music starts with the mother's lullaby,
and the further it is removed
from the home,
the less loving it becomes.

Healing, too, starts with the mother —
and can suffer the same fate.

Alone in the quiet
of my sanctuary,
I listen to
my neurones sing.

And then,
when you enter,
the new song
inspired by you.

What do you do?
They always ask.

But what matters
is not what —
but who.
Who am I
who is doing?

And I am best
in my room.

# The Quiet Place

*It is in quietness that we grow.*

DR. AINSLIE MEARES,
AUSTRALIA'S GREATEST PSYCHIATRIST

To incubate is to create an environment of optimal conditions for growth and development, for example, of an egg, a baby, of new ideas — and of health.

Incubation was an extremely popular means of therapy in ancient times.

"Incubation denotes the practice common among the Greeks and Romans of sleeping within the precincts of a temple for the purpose of receiving a dream vision of the healing god, who would reveal a remedy for the sleeper's sickness or trouble."

And not only in ancient times. It was still so employed in Welsh churches into the last century.

The word *incubate* comes from the Latin *cubare*, to lie down, hence to lie down in a healing place, a temple.

To the temple the sufferer came, desirous of cure. And in the Quiet Place he would lie down and await the cure from the god, from the Muse within him. And many were so cured. In fact, it is the only cure.

*So we sit and are quiet*
*In the calm and the stillness.*

MEARES

I would like my room to be such a Quiet Place. Like a temple, or a womb: "an encompassing protective space."

May I create a Quiet Place where at last the sufferer can find Peace, where he can feel safe to grow and develop. Where he can Know the Belovedness of his mother as The Mother.

———

*All that matters is to be one with the living God*
*to be a creature in the house of the God of Life.*

D. H. LAWRENCE

My mother was my God of Life,
I her creature.
Her house, her sphere of love,
the temple I re-enter
to be healed by incubation.

The truest incubation
is the sufferer
entering the temple
that is the healer.

To be a temple
within which
everyone may worship.
And to see everyone
as a temple for me.

I must become
a pure temple
fit for incubation.

# From Profane To Fane

*Nor sleep, nor sanctuary nor fane.*

SHAKESPEARE

*F*rom the Indo-European root *dhes* is derived the Greek *theos*, hence *theism* and *enthusiasm*.

From it also came the early Latin *fasnom*, a consecrated place, which later became *fanum*, a temple. From this we have the English word *fane*, a temple.

And from it was also derived *profane*, the *pro-* originally meaning in front of, or outside. Hence someone profane was outside the temple, not yet ready for admission.

Profane is defined as a disregard for sacred things; not sacred but worldly. Very similar is *secular*, worldly rather than spiritual.

In this sense, a profane person is one yet to embrace the spiritual, and this is the root cause of his suffering.

And to alleviate it, he needs to enter into the temple, to progress from the profane to the fane.

In his study of Confucius, Herbert Fingarette stated that the essence of his teaching was, as the subtitle puts it, Confucius — the Secular as Sacred. The ideal being "a life in which human conduct can be intelligible in natural terms and yet be attuned to the sacred, a life in which the practical, the intellectual and the spiritual are equally revered and are harmonized in the one act."

It is my intention, as best I can, to help you and me to the state of higher development, where our lives are sacred rather than secular, where we embrace the spiritual values as well as the worldly, where we cease to be profane.

May this process start for us here, now, in my home — in what, through our efforts, may one day become a fane.

———

Whether a place
is a temple,
depends not on its size,
but on whether
it induces Aspiration.

Let us work together
to make this little space
a temple for healing.

My Inner Temple
is a sacred place
within me,
consecrated
with the spirit
of my mother.

Before you arrive,
I try to expand it
through me,
out of me,
to encompass
all my home.

# From Temple To Sanctuary

*The deepest and most intimate sanctum of the soul.*

JUNG

*A*s you can see, I use the word *temple* quite frequently and in several contexts. Let's take a small trip through the word and some of its synonyms to see if we can find one more suitable in terms of healing.

Temple is derived from the Indo-European root *tem*, to cut. Hence the Latin *templum*, a temple or shrine; an open space for observation. The original meaning was a place cut out, a cutting, a clearing, for the purpose of augury. It was, according to Joseph Shipley in *The Origins of English Words*, "a stretch of land set aside by the augurs, to observe the stars."

A note on *augur.* It comes from the Indo-European root *aug*, to increase. Hence the Latin *auger,* a diviner, he who obtains divine favor, and thus increases, by his ability to foretell the future. From the same root comes *authority*— one who has the power to foretell.

So a temple was a clearing where the stars were observed for the purposes of divination. And that word is from the Indo-European root *deiw*, to shine, hence "sky, heaven, god." And our word *divine* is from the Latin *divinus,* foreseeing.

In the templum, the diviner saw the heavens, and God. Thus the templum itself became divine. Hence our definitions such as, "a building dedicated to worship" and "something regarded as having within it a divine presence."

The word *temple* does suffice, but I would prefer one that related not so much to the structure, but to the holy activity taking place within it. And I would also prefer one that had a richer history, referring more to holiness than to divination.

What now of some of its synonyms?

*Shrine* is not right for us, as it is "the tomb of a venerated person, such as a saint". It comes from the Latin *scrinum,* a case for books, hence it is "a container ... for sacred relics." Each of us can be a temple, but hardly a shrine — we are still alive.

What of *chantry?* I like it because of its derivation from the French *chanter,* to sing. It is a chapel, but one endowed by a benefactor to have masses and prayers said for him — not for everyone.

*Oratory?* "A place for prayer, such as a small private chapel." From the Latin *orare,* to pray. But, like chantry, it has too many religious encumbrances to be useful in a broader setting.

*Chapel* is preferable, for one definition is "a place of worship not belonging to an established church." But it is derived from the Latin *cappa,* a hooded cloak. Too introverted, too solitary.

What of *sanctum*? "A sacred or holy place." More so, "a special holy place within a temple". From *sak,* to sanctify, from which is also derived *sacred, consecrate, saint* and, of course, *sanctify.* This seems much better.

And *sanctuary:* "a sacred place," and also, "a place of refuge or asylum."

Sanctus, sanctus, sanctus

What was my mother? A sanctum, yes — but, even more so, a sanctuary. She was the sacred place within which I sought refuge, and where I felt sanctified. As I still do whenever I choose to re-enter her. She may be physically dead, but she lives, as long as I will, as the sacred relic in my Sanctum Sanctorum.

Each of us can be such a sanctuary, and so, of course, must be the healer — opening to take the sufferer into his Sanctum Sanctorum, his Holy of Holies.

*Thou hast unveiled thy inmost sanctuary.*

SHELLEY

———

It's much easier
to make my home
a sanctuary
— because it is my home.

*I* have long considered whether to have shoes worn in my room. Not because it is holy ground, but because I, and I hope you, would like it to be.

> *Put off thy shoes from thy feet, for the place*
> *whereon thou standest is holy ground.*
>
> EXODUS 3:5

> *The sandals or shoes which have been in*
> *contact with common ground must not be*
> *brought into contact with sacred ground.*
>
> HASTINGS,<br>ENCYCLOPAEDIA OF RELIGION AND ETHICS

The taking off should be a sign, a statement, of our intention — of our Aspiration.

It can be a prelude to our prayer on entering. No, more than that — it can be the prayer itself.

———

$\mathcal{I}$ would like to think of our prayer on entering as being an introit — verses sung at the entrance into the sanctuary.

How to keep the singing going after leaving the sanctuary?

One way is to make wherever you stand a sanctuary — to continually and constantly consecrate the common ground, and all upon it.

———

On a flight from Los Angeles to Sydney, a little old man was seated next to me. As soon as we had taken off, he placed a blanket over his head like a prayer shawl and went into a deep sleep, waking up only after at least eight hours.

He told me that he was a retired engineer for KLM and spent most of his life now traveling around the world on a special pass which entitled him to pay only ten percent of the airfare.

And he did this, he said, to show people all over the world the Glory of God.

He opened his little case — he was allowed to have only hand luggage — and took out a Hasselblad camera and a largish book. In it were glorious photographs he had taken in many countries, and opposite each, in five languages and many colored inks, he had composed a spiritual statement about it.

A man of humility, of peace, and of love.

He went on to tell me that he had to be able to sleep everywhere — on planes, on trucks and buses, at airports where sometimes he had to wait up to three days for the right cheap connection.

"I can sleep anywhere," he proclaimed. "I just listen to the music of the engines."

"And," he could have added, "I sing the Music of Life."

And in our sanctuary we try to listen to the Music, and sing It.

———————

May you,
in this room,
receive an intimation
of your mother
most loving:
of her Peace,
her Comfort, and Love.

If, when you leave,
you feel Beloved,
then the room
will have done
its work.

*Thou art one with her, and knowest not of self in thy supreme joy.*

BLAKE

$\mathcal{M}$y intense belief is that the root cause of all human suffering is not feeling loved, initially and most importantly, by our mothers — and later by all the others in the world who represent her.

This unlovedness comes about because of the extreme difficulties of the mother to fully and constantly manifest her deepest desire, her Maternal Instinct, this supreme expression of the drive for Life — the supreme altruistic expression of what Freud called the Eternal Eros.

And her difficulties came from her herself not feeling beloved by her own mother. And so it has gone on, transmitted down through succeeding generations.

The answer for you is to find the Love that she so wanted — and wants still — to give you. To go deep within her, to the Godness that is her.

And then, the love you now reciprocate to your mother, helps her to feel beloved by her own mother. For the child is, in the mother's unconscious, also, in part, the mother's mother. When the baby smiles back to its mother, it is the mother's own mother beloving her.

It is with this very much in mind, and in heart, that I have tried to structure and consecrate my home, and within it my room, so as to actuate in you, and in me, a remembrance of our mothers at their most loving.

For only then will our suffering be finally alleviated.

———

It all comes down
to seeing at last
our mothers as Love,
as the mothers
they wanted to be;
and us then
reciprocating reflexively.

From my hands
he feels
his mother's love.

Then into them,
her sphere of Love,
he radiates his
in grateful return.

It's not what I do
that matters,
but what I help you
to do:
to go into my heart
as a way to your mother's.

The difference between a healer and a sufferer is that the healer first opens his heart to his mother's love, whereas the sufferer first opens his to the healer — *as if* to his mother's love. The only difference is the "as if."

The healer to the sufferer, *as if* he were the healer's mother. And the sufferer to the healer *as if* he were the sufferer's mother.

All healing is this "as if."

———————

Your heart problem
is you feel
unloved.

I can only help you
if I myself
already feel
beloved.

Come into my room,
into the love
of my mother.

Her Belovedness
bestowed
on me,
and so on you.

*This is the matrix in which mind unfolds.*

HENRY GEORGE

To make my home a sanctuary for the suffering.

Mother — womb,
mater — matrix.

The English word *matrix* is from the Latin *mater* and is a synonym for the womb; and, relatedly, a containing place where something originates, is bred and develops — our Knowledge of her Love, and our consequent desire to reciprocate It to her, and to the world as her.

My wish is to make my home such a matrix.

The cure
is to enter
the Womb of Love.

———

My room to be
a sphere of love,
as when inside
our mothers.

Men, too,
can have a womb,
a blessed place
of loving containment.

In the heart,
and then
out into the home,
and then beyond
ever expanding
the sphere of love.

*Room — womb.*

Unconsciously,
so much the same,
and they sound
so much the same.
But the etymologists
tell us no.

But long ago
there was a time
when *oom* was
a container of love.

Say it, feel it
— and imagine.

My first task:
to realize
that the world
is the womb
of the Mother of Love.

And my second:
to so act
so that others
may realize it,
too.

I can never
have a womb.
But I can have
the heart
of a mother.

I expand my self
into the world
to encompass all
in my womb.

In Maori, *kopu* is a womb; *kopuka*, a small house.

Come into my room, my *kopuka*, to find again the peace within the *kopu* of your mother most loving.

———————

As we slip
into sleep,
we re-enter
the womb.

May you,
in this room,
dream of love.

*Nourished in the womb of pia mater.*

SHAKESPEARE

*I* place my hands on your head to comfort you, and "pia mater" comes to mind.

*Pia*, the Latin for tender, affectionate, devout, faithful.

*Mater*, mother.

According to Field and Harrison's *Anatomical Terms*, the pia mater is "the innermost of the three membranes which cover the central nervous system. . . It is an affectionate mother to the brain, protecting and nourishing it."

My hands as pia mater for you,
my room as pia mater for me.

_____

Her womb
is warmed
by her heart
— aflame.

The Greek word *thymos*, which we may translate as Life Energy, comes from the Indo-European root *dheu*, to rise into flames.

The altarlike elevation in the center of the orchestra of a Greek theater was called the *thymele*, and sacrificial incense was burned in the *thymiaterion*, or censer.

We each have a *thymele*, the chest, within which is the *thymiaterion*, the heart, filled with burning incense — the flames of Aspiration rising ever higher as the Life Energy increases.

I try to imagine my room as such an altar and us as censers, burning with Aspiration.

Aspiration
is the soul's yearning
for the More,
which is
the Highest.

———

I can write,
and talk, and teach,
but without the Feeling
in my chest –
it's all only words.

First I get the brazier
glowing in my chest,
then put a hot coal
wherever needed.

My every breath
flames the furnace
of the fiery forge
in which Aspiration
is wrought into reality.

My heart
a blazing fire
that attracts
the lost, cold
creatures
of the night.

My heart
a flaming beacon
for the sufferer
lost in distress.

My heart
a roaring campfire
of food,
of friendship,
of song.

Please come closer.




Come into my heart.
Feel the flame!

*Is there no balm in Gilead, no physician there?*

JEREMIAH 8:22

*I* once considered burning incense in my room, in part to declare I was not a doctor. But, even apart from the ecological considerations, I chose not to, for any single vibration imposes a limitation, contains the Imagination.

But if I now did choose to, which one would I burn?

Balm.

It was "much prized for its medical properties . . . soothing pain or healing wounds. . . . a healing, soothing, or softly restorative, agency or influence."

Thus, to balm means to soothe, to alleviate suffering — my therapeutic aspiration.

Sometimes when there is great suffering in my room, I imagine smelling it — even anointing with it.

———

*The balms that passion's wounds assuage.*

CRABBE

*Some burn damp faggots, others may consume*
*The entire combustible world in one small room.*

YEATS

58

My heart aflame!

As a man,
I put its heat
into you.

As a woman,
I encourage you
to come to it.

Warm yourself,
heal yourself,
inside me.

Come into my sphere.
Let us sanctify it
with the love
we will mutually create.

# Love Is Always Mutual

*M*utual means "having the same relationship each to the other. Directed and received in equal amount."

So often I hear the lover's complaint, "I love him more than he loves me." But I don't believe it's true. I've come to the opinion that love does not dwell within each person; it exists between them, has been created by the two of them, mutually, equally.

If he loves her only twenty units, then she also loves him but twenty units, too. But, she protests, I love him more — one hundred units. Not so — the sum total of their mutual love is this twenty units. But what of her extra eighty units? Only fantasy — and for this she is crying now they have parted.

When I speak of love, it is always with this understanding of its mutuality. It is not that he loves his wife, as such, or that she loves him. But rather that between them they have created a love of a certain size and character. Each of them — together, mutually, reciprocally. And they, together, will, I hope, nurture it with their desire to love, causing it to grow and develop.

I speak of the healer loving the sufferer. But this is only fantasy, and thus ineffective, unless the sufferer also contributes equally to the love between them.

And this is the task of the healer: through his therapeutic aspiration, his desire to create love with the sufferer, to actuate the same desire, equally, in him.

The cure will be the mutual love that they both have brought into being.

St. Francis kissed the leper and he was healed. But it was not due to his love as such, for there was initially no love between them — for the leper did not love St. Francis. His desire to love the leper was actuated by his compassion on beholding him. And the leper's desire to love St. Francis was then actuated by the kiss.

The cure was in the mutual love they both equally created.

Love is mutual trust
when most vulnerable:
hearts wide open
to one another —
like in the true Therapy
that alone can heal.

———

*As we all breathe together, we become one in thought and being.*

DR. ROBERT FULFORD

When I try to think of a perfect marriage my mind goes back to an old couple I knew many years ago. I used to be fascinated watching them sitting side by side in their armchairs, both gazing silently into the fire.

And then, quite abruptly, without a word, they both would rise to go to bed. Simultaneously, as if they were reading each other's thoughts, as I'm sure they were.

I've always imagined that they were so close to each other that they were breathing in perfect synchrony. Breathing as one.

And I recommend this when lying beside a loved one: synchronize your breathing and, thus, your soul.

Sometimes I do this with a sufferer, and I'd like to do it more. Just silently sit side by side, me synchronizing my breathing with his. Breathing sympathetically.

Even better is when we both synchronize our breathing, each reaching into the other, into his soul, to be one with him. Mutual Breathing. The union, the yoga, of our souls.

In a Quiet Place we can breathe together, mutually.

Know me
as your Self.

---

*It* is better not to think of giving and/or receiving love, but rather that True Healing is a steady state of love that comes to exist between us — each giving and receiving mutually and simultaneously.

We are both within the sphere of love that we both have created.

> Together,
> we spin
> our cocoon.

But we must always remember that the love is always mother-surrogate.

> True Healing
> is a circle
> as if between
> two loving mothers:
> he as mine,
> and me as his.

———

A man shows his love
by reaching out,
entering into the other.

A woman
by encouraging
the reaching out,
the entering into her.

A man heals
from his heart,
but a woman heals
into hers.

# Mutual Worship

*W*orship is the adoration, the ardent devotion, the reverent love, accorded to a deity or a sacred object.

Ananda, life as supreme Joy, I am told, is the worship of all, of everything.

And our worship must start with our mothers, as must theirs of us.

Mother and child: both Spiritual Beings. Both the objects of adoration. Mutual worship.

---

I open my arms
to give you  love,
to help you feel
beloved.
And then into them
to receive your love
in return.

Healing is this
mutual Belovedness.

# The Healer The Mother

It is in the nature of man to go into, to put into; and in the nature of woman to accept, to reach out, to take into.

Over the years, I have become more feminine in my practice. For example, I used to put my hands on the sufferer, directing energy into him. Now I keep off his body, in his aura, encouraging him, his energy, to come out into my waiting hands.

Strong male types make good treaters, good technicians. But the soft woman is the healer. Come to me, let me enfold you.

The Best Samaritan is the mother.

———

Comfort ye,
Comfort ye, my darling,
saith your Mum.

The voice of him
that crieth
in the wilderness
was me
in my cot.

And always
she came
and comforted.

The Wise One knows
that her body
is a healing temple,
and encourages us
to enter.

Going inside another
heals him less
than helping him
to come into you.

As a man,
I made music
to enter you
to heal.

Now,
as a woman,
I want you
to sing to me,
to enter into me.


Is there music
in my home?
Of course!
That's A Plenty!

And I try to make it
the True Music
that heals –
like from the mother
into her womb.

I live in
her sphere of Love.
Into it
she radiates hers,
and from it
I radiate mine
back to her.

Healing
is encouraging
the sufferer
to enter into
the healer.

Not me
out from my heart,
but you
into it.

The art of healing
is to encourage
the sufferer's entry
into the healer's
inner temple.

The healer
must make himself
a pure Temple
that the sufferer
can safely enter.

*W*hy do I use the word *sufferer* rather than *patient* which is from the Latin *patior*, I suffer?

A patient dissociates himself from the healing process — he wants the healer to do it for him, like leaving his car with the mechanic. Whereas a student wants to be taught how to heal himself.

Both the patient and the student are sufferers, for, as the Buddha taught, all our lives are suffering. Hence the one word suffices for both. However, the sufferer who is aware of his suffering and wants to overcome it is not a patient but a student.

Why the word *student*?

The word is derived from the Indo-European root *steu*, to push. From this comes the Latin *studere*, to push on, and *studium*, application, zeal.

The student zealously pushes on to learn. So, unlike the patient, only the student ever graduates out of suffering.

———

The ancient sufferers
did not enter
the temple of Asklepios,
but entered Asklepios
as the temple.

# The Sufferer Seeking Asylum

"*If* the therapist makes some moment of life hold enough safety . . . the integrative factor can operate." So wrote Dr. Louis Cholden.

Asylum is the protection offered by a sanctuary. From the Greek *asulon*, sanctuary. And a sanctuary is a place of refuge, of safety — from the Latin *sanctus*, sacred.

So the True Therapist needs to provide a sanctuary for the sufferer, to grant him asylum. That, in this place of peace, he may at last heal himself.

For this reason I work not in a cold commercial office, but in my home; trying as best I can to make it a sanctuary. Hoping that one day they may say of me:

*Beneath his Roof They found asylum oft.*

BYRON

―――――――

Come into
my home,
Come into
my room,
Come into
me.

Healing is my life,
and I can't separate it
into business
and domestic.
I live at home,
so that's where I do
my life's work.

*Most systematizers in relation to their systems are like a man who builds an enormous castle and himself lives alongside it in a shed; they themselves do not live in the enormous systematic building. But in the realm of mind and spirit this is and remains a decisive objection. Spiritually understood, a man's thoughts must be the building in which he lives — otherwise the whole thing is deranged.*

KIERKEGAARD

*W*ell, my system's certainly not "an enormous castle," but it has become an edifice, growing larger.

And I hope I don't live "alongside it in a shed." Rather I live, I believe, in this home, and in it I need you. For it is my desire to help you, and yours to want me to, that may cause my home to become more a castle than a shed.

Through our work together in my home, may my "whole thing" not become "deranged," but more enlightened.

---

A commercial office
is for strangers,
a healer's home
for friends.
Please come in.

A commercial office
is at best a house,
but never a home.

$\mathcal{D}$oing my work in my home makes it harder for me to split into office-angel, house-devil.

You see me in my home as I really am. And, unlike the psychoanalyst, this is how I want you to see me — realistically.

For, through accepting me as I really am, you come at last to accepting yourself.

Reality, the cure,
starts when the healer
is seen as himself.

————

The bigger the building,
the heavier the overheads.
The heavier the overheads,
the less the desire
to heal.

There comes a time
when their weight
collapses
the structure of healing.
Only jagged ruins
remain
— as treatment.

The conductor Sir Thomas Beecham, himself no miniaturist, used to complain about the inflated modern symphony orchestras and choirs used nowadays to perform Handel, disparaging them as "those large executive forces."

This thought came to me at a concert. All those executive forces: the composer, his publisher and his printer; the music distributors, licensees and hirers. And all their accountants and bankers and lawyers. The conductor and the musicians, and all their accountants and bankers and lawyers and agents; the concert hall owners and managers, their assistants, and publicists, and ticket sellers, and ushers, and cleaners, and stage hands. And all their accountants, etc. And the entrepreneur. And the orchestral management . . . and on and on.

All those forces — for what? To make a change inside me, and the other me's.

But what change? Never one that matters. For although music has life-enhancing spiritual powers, to so uplift the audience is never the intention of all those forces.

All that out there brings about little spiritual change inside me.

But what if all those forces were actually designed to produce such a change?

I gaze around me, and upward, in Westminster Abbey, in the cathedrals at Wells and Exeter, at Stonehenge. Am I really experiencing a spiritual change? Am I filled with aspiration? Am I uplifted? Not superficially, momentarily — but deeply. Really?

I contemplate the vaults, the altars, the icons, and place my hand over my heart. All that going on out there to produce the change inside here.

And it fails — must fail. For all of it encourages me to go outside my self, into the cathedral. Whereas the spiritual path is inward, to the God within.

We don't need large executive forces for healing — in fact, they vitiate it. No orchestras, no cathedrals. Just a touch, a smile, and a lullaby.

My room is not a cathedral, not even an executive suite. But, as best I can, I have designed it for us both to make a change inside here.

————

*I have a room.*
*'Tis poor, but 'tis my best, if Thou wilt come*
*Within so small a cell, where I would fain*
*Mine and the world's Redeemer entertain.*
*I mean my heart.*

SIR MATTHEW HALE

I am my room.
May it, I,
someday become
like Hale's.

A healer can only
give his all,
passionately,
intensely,
when he knows
the walls
will resonate
sympathetically.

# The Familiar Setting

*B*ack in my psychiatry days, I once remarked to a colleague that I found it more difficult to make a diagnosis in a strange setting, say at a bedside in an unfamiliar hospital, rather than in my office.

He replied that he didn't understand me. Everywhere was the same for him.

Then I went on to state that it was even more difficult if I had a cold.

"Rubbish!" he rejoined. "Why should that be a problem? You just take a history, then add up the points to make the diagnosis."

I shook my head, puzzled. "Somehow I don't work that way."

Years later, psychiatry thankfully behind me, a healer gave me the answer. "Don't you realize he was working by formulae. But you're a healer — you work by feel."

And I still do — and always will — for the heart is the organ of feelings.

And it is much easier to feel in a setting that is quiet, and peaceful — and familiar.

> A treater
> goes by
> measurement,
> but a healer
> by feel.

———————

Cures only come
to those with
a green thumb.

And my thumbs
are greener
in my own garden.

The holistic therapist
brings to the sufferer
all he has learned
that makes him whole.

I bring to you
a capacious library
of the Greats.

# My Familiars

**Familiar:** an attendant spirit.

> See on my shelves
> all the Greats
> in their books —
> my familiars
> to assist me
> to alleviate your suffering,
> as they have helped me
> on the way
> to alleviate mine.

We are in a room filled with spirits who will assist me to help you.

Let us take them into us.

My work is to enable you to be one so inspired.

———

*The Soul . . . settles in some room*
*where it may best . . . sway the whole body.*

NATHANIEL FAIRFAX

*Elysium is as far as to*
*The very nearest Room.*

EMILY DICKINSON

*Thus methinks should men of judgement frame*
*Their means of traffic from the vulgar trade,*
*And, as their wealth increaseth, so enclose*
*Infinite riches in a little room.*

M<small>ARLOWE</small>

*Since I am coming to that holy room,*
*Where, with thy choir of saints forevermore,*
*I shall be made thy music; as I come*
*I tune the instrument here at the door,*
*And what I must do then, think here before.*

DONNE

$\mathcal{I}$ once read that the way to choose a good school was to observe the students leaving at the end of the day. Whether they burst out, as if released from prison, or just left leisurely — or, better, invigorated.

I have thought of this many times since when observing sufferers leaving a practitioner's room. Are they more energized, more alive, more loving, than when they entered? At best, they emerge from the treater's room as they went in, or often more devitalized. But from a healer's they come out alive anew.

Often while working in my room, I think of how the sufferer should look on leaving — like I was a good school.

———

My star signs
are fire,
and expansive.
Over the years
I've had to learn
to concentrate
my intensities —
all contained now
in this room,
focused onto us.

# The Watershed Experience

**Watershed:** a critical point that marks a major change of course; a turning point.

*A* mountain range is a watershed — there can be rain on one side and bright sunshine on the other. How to help the sufferer cross over the ridge?

Many years ago, I met a world-renowned pianist sorely afflicted with cancer. I offered to do anything — everything — to help her. Most of all, I suggested I would rent a cottage by the sea and work with her, be with her, for as long as it took for her to turn herself around — to embrace Life. She arranged to come at the end of her concert tour, but she succumbed before then.

Ever since I have been obsessed with the idea of therapy as a watershed experience: the sufferer staying as long as is needed to bring about a permanent change. Until he can proclaim, with the deepest conviction, I will never again be as I was before. I have passed the turning point. I have crossed over the bridge. I am changed — permanently. I embrace Life. I am ready to walk out into — run out into — the sunlit Garden of Life.

There must be no time limitation — staying for however long until the critical point has been passed. Perhaps a few hours, perhaps . . . who knows?

And all the time working toward this permanent change. With the strongest intention.

The sufferer must set out with this strong intention. The journey to the healer's sanctuary must be like an odyssey. His goal always clearly before him: I want to change. I will change.

All the things that I do are designed to help the sufferer cross over to the sunlit side. And I try to make even a brief contact at least a mini-watershed.

———

# How Long Is A Session?

*W*ho says a therapeutic session should be of a certain length? Ten minutes, twenty, forty, fifty — two hours? A day? A week? More? Less?

To quite an extent, the length of time allotted is determined by the image — for example, a psychiatrist usually devotes fifty minutes. And if I'm not careful, I still do that today, although my psychiatric days are past.

There can be no fixed time. The sufferer should stay until his suffering is relieved — however long that may turn out to be. Completely unpredictable — and so it should be.

How long does a session last? How long will it take you to change?

A mountaineer ascends the steep face step by step, hammering a piton firmly into the rock to support him for each step on his progress. Piton by piton — each one secure, so he will never fall back.

How long will it take?

It depends on the mountaineer and the mountain.

How long will it take you to ascend to the top?

It all depends on you and your mountain.

Just concentrate on making each step a secure, permanent change.

And when you leave, don't think of what I've done, or even what we've done, but what has happened, what has come to us.

And whatever you think it may be — accept it. For Acceptance leads to Gratitude, and Gratitude to feeling Beloved. And Belovedness is the only cure for suffering.

Try to remember that what befalls us is always Belovedness, for That is all of Existence.

> Don't come
> for a fixed time,
> come to spend time.
> Come to visit.
> And leave,
> not by the clock,
> but by the heart.

———————

Although in the preceding pages I have spoken somewhat physically of home and hearth, that is not the ultimate sense in which I mean them.

Home is wherever we feel loved by our mothers — and this can be anywhere, everywhere.

And every place can be a hearth. We just need to consecrate it with a burning coal from our hearts aflame.

And then the healer's presence, openhearted, arms outstretched, itself will be a sanctuary.

———

When a baby,
the whole world was your mother
— as it still is,
and always will be.
Everyone is but an aspect
of your mother,
as is your healer.

I encourage you to see me
as the loving mother,
that you may feel Beloved by her.
For This is the only cure
for human suffering.

# A Time to Sit on the Yellow Sands?

*To fix my gaze through the eternal light*
*Until I had seen all that I could see!*

DANTE

And Blake!

*To my Friend Butts I write*
*My first Vision of Light*
*on the yellow sands sitting*

. . . . . . . . . . . . . . . . . . . . . .

*Such the Visions to me*
*Appeard on the Sea*

Why do so many blessed individuals speak of the light? Is the mystical experience a birth? From the dark of the womb into the light of the world?

Perhaps, it is the Time for me fix my gaze through the eternal light.

Maybe,
a Time will come
when the sufferer and I
will just sit together,
silent,
on the yellow sands.

———

Dr. John Diamond graduated from Sydney University Medical School in 1957 and obtained his Diploma of Psychiatric Medicine in 1962. He is a Fellow of the Royal Australian and New Zealand College of Psychiatry and a Member of the Royal College of Psychiatrists of Great Britain.

After practicing psychiatry in Australia, he came to the United States where he expanded into Complementary Medicine, becoming President of the International Academy of Preventive Medicine. As he became more involved with the concept of Life Energy, he increasingly concentrated on the enhancement of the sufferer's Life Energy so as to actuate his own innate Healing Power.

A musician, composer, poet, author and photographer, he has over many years employed Creativity, especially the High Arts, regarding it as an essential and major component of Healing.

His concept of holism is based on his extensive experience in psychiatry, medicine, the humanities, the arts, and healing.

The Diamond Center is dedicated to his principles of Holistic Healing.

For further information, please write to:

*The Diamond Center*
*P. O. Box 381*
*South Salem, New York 10590 USA*